# My Healing Bible

## Healing my Haunted Houses

## Dedication

This Book is dedicated to my sons Tyler, Amir, and Amari, for without the love of you there would be no me. Healing the Haunted Houses in me is so that the cycles Don't repeat itself. Its time to be free for me, you and my grandchildren Travis, Chance, and Tobias.

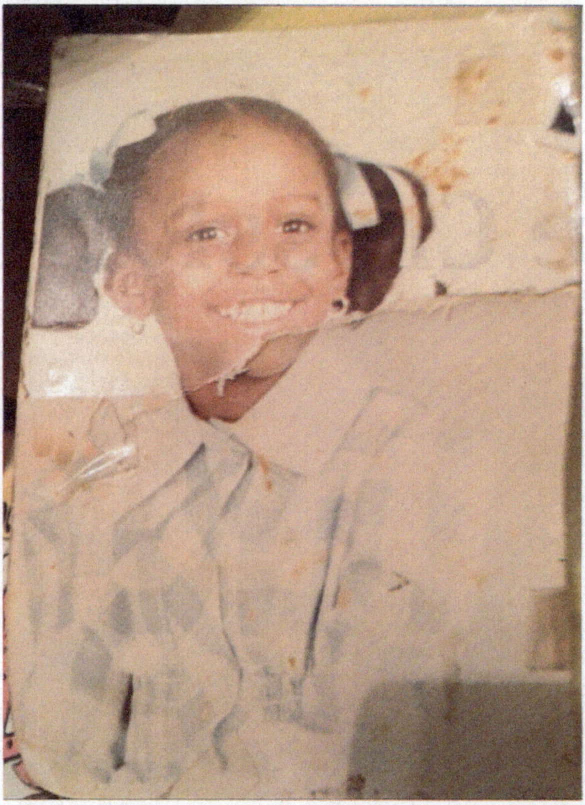

# The CrossROADS

Here I Am in the second stretch of my life. I'm currently at a place often referred to as one of life's crossroads. I feel like we stand at various crossroads of during significant milestones in our journey - our twenties, thirties, forties and so forth. At each point we stand at halt, often feeling stagnated, staring at the many street signs of life trying to figure out what's next. We often find ourselves standing at the crossroads of life trying to figure out and navigate through this thing called LIFE.

During the first part of my life's journey, I spent many moments trying to find my footing, or should I say my place in this world which I served me a plate full of LIFE LESSONS leaving me THIRSTY for a PEACE of mind in a world that didn't quite Love me back. After MANY PLATES of LIFE LESSONS, that left me MALNOURISHED and empty inside at times, I set out on a quest to fill my EMPTY plates up with a SPIRITUAL Peace of mind.

In my first book, My Love Affair with Love: Finding Peace Through the Pain (published in December 2018), I had the blessed opportunity to share some of my life HEALING journey. My search for peace and self-love, led me to self-reflection on earlier segments of my life, from childhood recollections between the early ages of two and five saying my first words responding to another child at a birthday party who asked my age. I don't recollect my parents telling or practicing what my age was, it was a KNOWING that I knew. I remember that moment clear as day nearly 50 plus years later (I am sure you are not 50 plus so this sentence needs to be changed to reflect your age now). In my recollections I vividly remember looking at a tree, and without anyone EVER telling me, knowing the green and brown sticks protruding from it were called branches. It felt like God was TEACHING Me about the universe, teaching and grooming me to hear His voice. These memories remain stuck in my mind even til this day, without an understanding of how I knew those things, despite not one person explaining to me what I observed or said. I found out later in my journey that I would be connected to something bigger than me, that this entity would be intangible to me, but I had to trust where it was trying to lead me. There would be some necessary tearing down and rebuilding of my Spiritual foundation. I had to encounter LIFE first and stand at many, many crossroads while allowing God to introduce me to the world, a world where I could finally start to experience that thing called PEACE. I longed to embrace PEACE before transitioning to be with THE MOST HIGH. Saying R.I.P. at the end of life, started not to fit well with me, I want to experience RESTING IN PEACE while I was alive.

In my first book, mentioned above, I took readers on a nostalgic journey, beginning as a five-year-old little girl named Tracy ending as a 24-year-old mother giving birth to my first son. I shared the trials and tribulations I endured in my first part of my journey, including various love affairs-some painful, some joyful.

Many of my Love Affairs blossomed, a couple consisted of longing to belong to something or someone. Wanting to be attached to what I call my ultimate fairy tale relationship, which didn't quite work as I had planned. That fairy tale came with a painful price to my mind, to my body and my soul. God had other plans for me in that area, I also spoke about some my happy Love Affairs, like my Love Affair with music. Music is where I zone out into one my happy places. Music provided an escape to a peaceful state of mind through telling lyrical stories through its melodies and instruments. I'm a lover of all types of music and of many genres. Let's just say my Love Affair's Journey with music wasn't based on a relationship with another person. This Love Affair was an Entanglement of Life Lessons and experiences, some were great and some not so great.

    After writing about my journey of finding peace during pain, the reception was overwhelmingly positive. It received great reviews which were a blessing. I was very, very nervous about how my first book would be received by others, therefore I am humbly grateful about the outcome of My Love Affairs with Love. Along with receiving great reviews and support of my first book, then came the ultimate question from my book supporters; "What's next?", meaning my book supporters wanted more. They want a sequel. Was there going to be more to come? They wanted the one-woman monologue. They wanted more of the journey that I took them on that was relatable. They wanted more of the nostalgic seeds that I planted along the way as they read each chapter. They wanted more from me! The requests made me feel very grateful. Their requests ignited a fire within me, driving me to explore ideas for a follow-up. I went full throttle trying to fulfill my book supporters' request to give them more of my JOURNEY to MY PEACE. The ideas in my head were all over the place. These creative ideas began blooming left and right as I set out to give the people what they wanted, yes! I'm getting ready to do some things. My mind was racing with all sorts of ideas.

I wanted to deliver something better and then my first book. I envisioned being a vessel helping others through their trauma, hidden pains, and healing process. I wanted to be THE VESSEL for encouragement, self-love, and healing. I LOVE to see people set free from their pains and hardships of life, which I waddled in for so long. When I got a glimpse of what being free felt like, I wanted others to experience and know that blessed feeling. So the zeal to deliver what the people wanted, resonated through my body giving me purpose, I felt on fire! I found something that I can do to help others in their process, a sense of purpose that I struggled to figure out. I knew deep down in my heart I wanted to help or serve others in some type of way especially with their healing processes. I was starting to find that footing, my place in this world that I was searching for during the first stretch of my journey, one of my many LOVE AFFAIRS. My love Affair with BELONGING.

    Then it happened, the fire inside me that wanted to give the people what they wanted, began to dwindle. Something inside me felt off. The momentum to start my next book faded. The flames within started slowly going faint, the light inside of me started to go dim. That fire that was once ignited started to burn out and stagnation started to set in my spirit. I was all over the place trying center myself and my thoughts on which route to take to get started on book #2. With so much uneasiness in spirit, I started to second guess my next move; by this time the fire went all the way out. I found myself standing at another crossroad.

Here I Am STUCK! not knowing what my next move should entail. Trying to figure out why I can't regain the momentum to get started on my next book. Where should I begin? What should I give the people? As I struggled to figure out my next move, life events continued to unfold, manifesting for me, that there were more life lessons and self-development brewing behind the scenes. God was looking at my life file and there were some blank pages that had to be filled in. Life and the universe weren't quite ready for me to unleash what was next for me. The Spirit revealed that releasing the book prematurely would be out of alignment. I couldn't give the people what they wanted until God gave what I needed to take place, more HEALING!

I needed more healing- physical, mental, spiritual, sexual soul-ties and so forth. God was breaking my OLD foundation to build a NEW and Healthier one. And when I tell you this process, although PAINFUL to be Broken down and RE-BUILT on God's foundation, was necessary and well worth it.

Then an Ah ha! Moment hit me. The Spirit revealed to me that one of the reasons causing the stagnation with getting book #2 birthed; I was currently Living in book #2. WHOA! The timing of birthing book #2 now would be a premature decision. When that Ah Ha moment occurred, it all started to make absolute sense. That Ah Ha moment also brought a sense of relief, because now I can free myself from the pressure of fulfilling an obligation to others wanting book #2 to be release ASAP! Don't get me wrong,

I will be forever grateful that the urgency for book #2 was in such great demand, due to the awesome reviews from Book #1; but, like I stated, I was currently living in the development of my next book and wanted book #2 to be even better than book #1. MORE relatable. I want it to be even more TRANSPARENT and VULNERABLE than I was before. I wanted book #2 to be a great vessel for HEALING! Excuse my French, there was no way I was going to deliver something half-ass. You CAN NOT HALF ASS HEALING. God was showing to stay attuned with ALIGNMENT, His timing and my timing has an absolute DIFFERENCE. God's watch ticks different from ours. His timing BLESSES and is conducive to your life PURPOSE.

So, as I ceased fire on the birthing book #2. As I struggled with what was next in my life. As the Spirit of The Most High had already revealed that I was living out book#2, here I was at the Crossroads of my journey on STUCK Blvd and WHAT'S NEXT Ave.

A year or so had passed and the anniversary date for book #1 came and went. In between time, while I waited, I hosted several book signings events, that did very, very well I must say. I also had the pleasure of speaking engagements where I met some wonderful people, and we shared our testimonies and healing process while supported each other's gifts. It has been amazing to see others on their HEALING grind; being that I felt alone as started my HEALING grind. There are times when God needs you to be Alone during the process so he can have you ALL to himself, teaching you to RELY solely on him without any outside distractions. It's not easy by far but necessary to teach to learn to his voice and directions reminding me of the importance of (which will be REPEATED to you all through this journey)... Just Trust in the Process.

As I stood at the crossroad, I started asking God what was next for me? What should I give to the people? For a while there was dead silence at the crossroads, I couldn't hear God's voice. I get frazzled when I can't hear The Most High's Voice. I learned when those moments occur, get still, and continue the process of TRUST in his plans. Within the Quietness his voice resonates, "Trust that I will NEVER leave you or Forsake you." HE IS THERE!

When you're standing at one of the crossroads of life, it can feel much like a chess game, pondering with much intensity on the next move you should take that would benefit your life journey. That part of life is filled with so many anxiety levels. Trying to quietly here from God. Trying to strategize your next move on the game board of Life. Like I stated, it feels like a game of chess. Sitting there trying not to second guess what your next move should entail or which way to go on the board game, I was stuck at that crossroad. Wondering what's the next move in trying to proceed in the right direction of being a vessel for others on their path in healing, while gaining more healing along the way.

Then it happened the SPIRIT said, "Take them back.", I was like what!?, First I had to make sure that I was hearing the SPIRIT inside speaking to me. It's that second guessing that we do in midst of asking The Highest, to direct our move in the game of life. Trust me all of us have experienced those second-guessing moments, so don't be hard on yourself when that occurs. Just keep Trusting in the Process. Amp up your FAITH FUEL, so when those moments happen, you'll will be more accustomed to getting quiet and asking The Most High, to make his directions for you clear.

Here's the thing we tend think that VOICE of direction will come BURSTING through the crevices of the walls with a Deep Godly tone, saying something like MY CHILD YOUR NEXT MOVE SHALL BE, like a scene from the Movie the Ten Commandment. I once heard Joel Osteen say that it feels like a gentle whisper. That's God way of speaking to your soul. You may not understand why the still gentle whisper is giving you some type of direction or thoughts. Your intellect will not understand it and Truth be told your Spirit man will not understand it. That gentle whisper within you is guiding you, you'll know it when it hits. It's a KNOWING voice, that's NOT YOUR VOICE. You just have TRUST in the PROCESS of the VOICE and the God that's in you. When I heard the Spirit VOICE saying take them back, I questioned what I had heard. I began to spend many months being quiet, letting life continue to do its thing, the answer began to become clearer and clearer on what the spirit Voice meant by take THEM BACK?

    It was on a very beautiful Saturday afternoon, I decided to take it easy that day. No running around. I remember I just wanted some ME TIME, just do ABSOLUTELY nothing. My Me time entailed door-dashing something delicious to eat, staying in my lounging wear and enjoying movies. I turn on Netflix, began scrolling the movie list. I stop at a sequel, of one of my favorite scary movies, Halloween. When the title sequence began, I did my Movie setup ritual, I set my air condition to the perfect temperature. There's nothing like the perfect hot/cold room during movie time. I got all my favorite snacks, drinks lined up in perfect order, call me weird but I'm a little order fanatic, and a tad bit O.C.D. I think most of us have some type of ritual that we like to do when we are setting up shop for peace time. I finally had everything set up for my peace time! I finally got all snuggled under the blankets, ready for Halloween, this all-time classic horror film. The Halloween Franchise has many movies under its belt, starting from 1978 to 2021. Call me crazy but I've watched every one of those films.

    As I scrolled through my choices trying to make my final decision of which Halloween flick to watch, I decided to go with a sequel and a remake of one of the Halloween movies. As the movie is rolling the title sequence, and first scene starts to roll, it was clear and apparent that the beginning of the film is taking you back to Micheal Myers' (one of the main characters of Halloween, along with Jamie Lee Curtis) earlier years of his life, giving you an outlook of his family dynamics and the dysfunction that Micheal was born into. The first scene takes place in the kitchen of Micheal Meyer's family home. You could clearly see the dysfunction that spurred through the cracks and crevices within the dwellings of the home, the spirit, and the aesthetics of the home of was gloomy and in a disarray. Micheal appeared detached, even at an early age. Micheal had other siblings which included an older sister, who right from the start is belittling Micheal showing absolutely no sibling love towards her brother. Micheal's mother displayed as much positive, nurturing love as she possibly could despite the high level of dysfunction roaming through the home. Then there was the boyfriend of the mother who clearly had no love nor positive connection with Micheal. You can see all types of generational curses radiating throughout the first few minutes of the film. Along with the character traits of Micheal Myers, as the movie revs up, you'll start to get a sense that Micheal's family dynamics played a huge part in Michael's personality and character dysfunctions. Micheal's disturbing behavior was also displayed at school with no real cultivation with any other students. He was even bullied by other students which fueled his rage even more. His dysfunction started evolving into torturing and killing animals, his raged spilled over into brutally killing a student. Being that I had watched the original Halloween movie, I wasn't necessarily scared of this movie, but more interested in what made Micheal truly snap. This is where it became clear. The Voice that kept telling me for a while, "TAKE THEM BACK!" I heard several times during the course of the movie and that voice started getting louder and louder, clearer and clearer "TAKE THEM BACK!", to the beginning of YOUR STORY! Your Pathology, Your DNA traits. My Parents would always say, If You don't know where you have been or come from, you won't know where to go.

Then it finally resonated in my soul as the movie continues to play out, that it's imperative to take my story back to the very beginning, the parts before I was conceived. I needed to find out my family dynamics, not only the parts where boy meets girl (my parents), I needed to go deeper into generational influences. It was imperative to do so, for my healing processes. I wanted to cleanse my soul of as much turmoil that I had experience in the first part of my journey. Don't get me wrong, not every part of my journey was full of bad times; for the most part my childhood was nice, it was the later years that were extremely challenging. You are talking about growing pains! Those growing pains also came with a lot of bumps, bruises, and tears. If you're willing to do the work there is healing and peace that I pray will start to fill those dark and painful places with a victorious and healthy new path, and it's happening GLORY BE TO GOD!

Now Let's get ready to take another Healing Journey ride with me, to one of my many sequels of my life story. Although my beginnings and journey weren't quite as gloomy and horrific as Micheal Myers', But there were some generational curses I need to continue to address, so that I could continue onward on my Healing journey to I Happier and Healthier version me. This reflection was vital for my healing process. Much like how Michael Myers' backstory in the Halloween movie franchise explained his behavior. I needed to understand my origins to cleanse my soul of turmoil.

Now as I take you all on this healing journey let's a little bit about God's timing that is an absolute part of the healing process. There are many, many more lessons, quizzes, and tests to partake in. Yes! I know. Who wants to continue with all these life lessons on so forth? But timing is a huge part of the alignment to healing. This is where you can start LIVING and RESTING IN PEACE on earth.

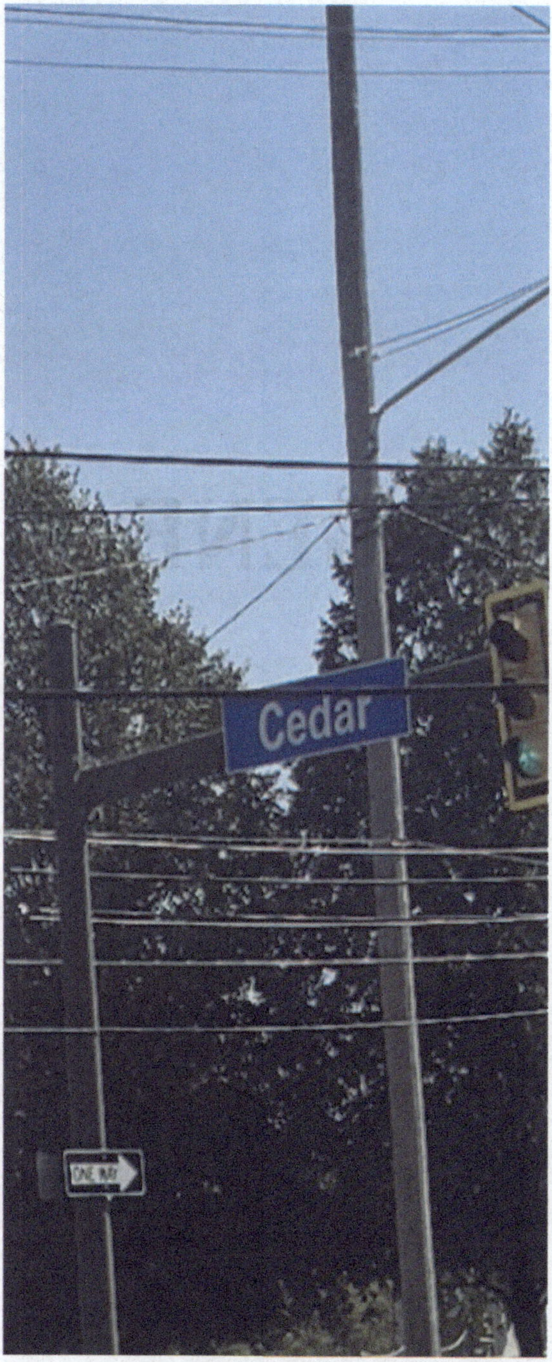
Cedar
ONE WAY

# My GENEsis

When we think of the word GENESIS we tend to think of the bible, where we find out about the development, the beginning & the birth of the world.

Like the first book of the Bible, GENESIS, everything has a beginning, a starting point, A BIRTHING- a seed that was planted in some type of way, to start your birthing process. There was a cultivation, a spiritual exchange that took place. That cultivation may have developed on bad or good soil, either way that cultivation was planted and ORDAINED to BIRTH the HUMAN. The Essence of YOU. Within this ESSENCE your GENE traits were manifested, you know your DNA development. The Human Development consists of two people or male and female consummating a human soul tie exchange…. SEX!

Let's talk about the parents (seed) of that birth =the Child(ren).

The female and male of the birth, consist of mother and a father =THE PARENTS. Within that exchange you inherited DNA from each parent.

**DNA**= (DEOXYRIBONUCLEIC (acid) is a molecule that contains the genetic information that controls the growth, development and reproduction of organisms.

DNA is found in cells of almost all organisms, including humans, and is passed from one generation to the next. In some cases, just because you have PARENTS, doesn't mean that you have a TRUE relationship with either or even know one or the other. You may have been adopted, orphaned or raised by family members and friends, whatever the case may be.

The DNA of the Parents and their journey can sometime explain the many reasons why you operate the way that you do, for instance, I have a friend who has never met her biological mom, yet she had this unknown desire to become a seamstress. When she was around fabric, clothing and even upholstery on furniture, or cloth of any sort, she would find herself drawn to those things. She began sewing and home decorating. She did not know why she had a desire to engage in such a career. She finally found the missing link of why it was embedded in her spirit to choose that career. She was at a friend's home improvement event as the guest speaker. After speaking, she began networking the room. She encountered a young lady that was very intrigued with her speech and her career. While engaging in a lengthy conversation, the two exchanged information for future business endeavors. The lady noticed a familiar last name on her business card. Upon asking a few questions, the guest speaker realized this was a cousin of her biological Mother, who gave her away to family member when she was ten months old. Her mom had encountered some mental breakdowns after she was born. Come to find out her mother and grandmother were both seamstresses. WOW! She hadn't even met her biological mother to even know that being a seamstress was already embedded in her DNA, which caused her to gravitate towards the LOVE of fabric and home decor. With all that being said the DNA components of both of ones parents along with your environmental upbringing, plays a part in some of your personality and character traits. The basis of your environmental foundation plays an absolute huge part in how you operate and move through this world either on a positive or negative foundation. Just like Micheal Myers, which I could clearly see in first few scenes of the movies, his household environment was a sheer setup for mental failure, genetic collapses with negative or positive character and personality interests.

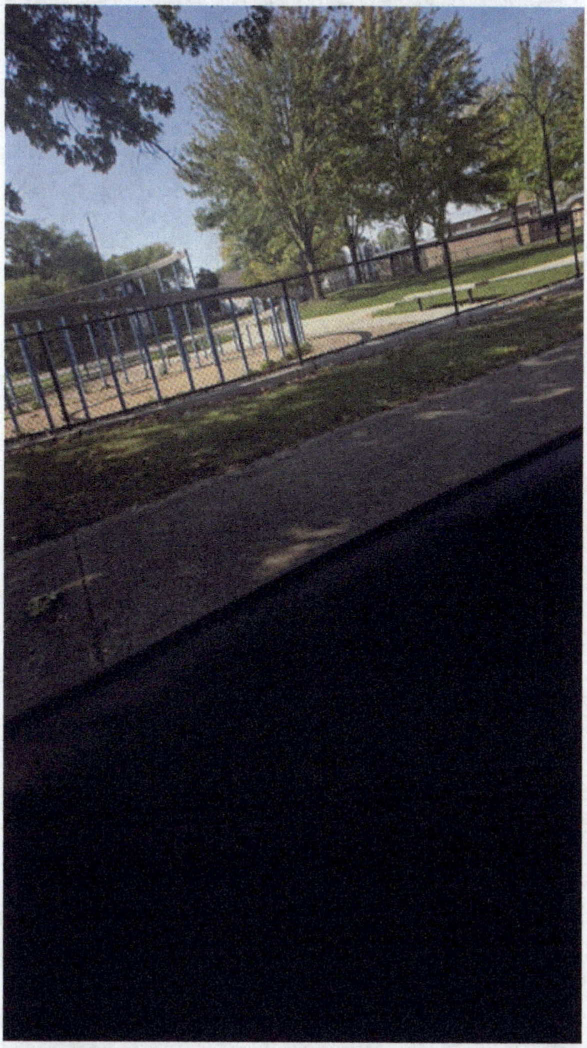

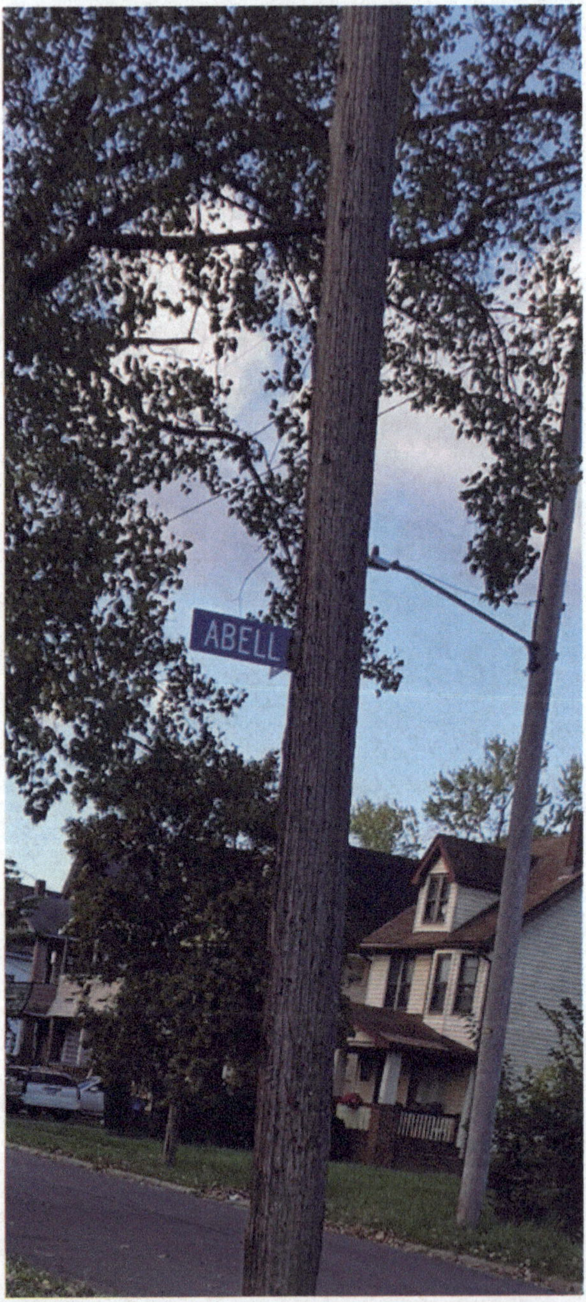
ABELL

There's a saying that, "Home is where the heart is." One's home should be a safe haven, their safe place away from a world that doesn't quite love you back. As a kid, I would watch television shows that displayed the idea of happy family dynamics. You know the shows that depicted the two parents, working dad and stay-at-home mother. White picket fence. their family home had all the aesthetics of a cozy and peaceful domicile. Everything was placed perfectly in every nook and cranny of the home. The children had all the modern amenities at their disposal making their childhood seem stress free and fun. The latest fashion. Toys on every shelf. The perfect bedroom layout and so forth. When the child(ren) on the television screen would get into mischief, a family forum (meeting) was held to discuss the repercussion and consequences of their bad behavior. When the episode would end, the reality of Life would set in again. That life for some people isn't quite like the shows on television. The Fantasy -vs -Reality of one's home front was much different in REAL LIFE! Reality for some people is their life didn't consist of the same dynamics that played out on the television screen. Their domicile wasn't as peaceful and filled with the same amenities the children had on T.V., The nooks and crannies of their four walls SCREAMED of dysfunction and chaos. The heart of their home needed some repairing. Their home wasn't their SAFE place, at times it was just as cruel as the outside world. For some of us escaping, into a fantasy of peace feels or looks like, imagining yourself as one those characters in the T.V. show where everything looks PERFECT.

    I will continue to remind you that, for the most part, my childhood was pretty decent. I had the pleasure of creating and experiencing some awesome memories with my family and yes I did come from a two parent home. I was blessed to have spent time with Grandparents on both my mother and father side. I had a spur of Uncles, Aunties, Cousins and I have a little sister. I enjoyed some fun memories with all of them. But like the good there were some bad and painful moments along the way observe on both sides of my family that would later affect my life path in some traumatic ways.

There was dismantling in my life journey which had to take place in my SOUL. There was some tearing down of my PERSONAL & SPIRITUAL home which had to be demolished and rebuilt on a HEALTHIER foundation so that I could break some generational curses in my DNA. I had to learn to reprogram my mind to learn the difference between REALITY and THE FANTASY of my life, that held me in bondage for a very, very long time.

Tearing down a house and rebuilding it requires blood, sweat and tears. I prayed many, many days and years that God would give me the tools and spiritual equipment to begin the work to start The RECONSTRUCTION OF ME and when I say that the demolishing process was very PAINFUL, to say the least, taking down the old and broken bricks of me was not an overnight process.

My spiritual HOME and Personal Homes were screaming for Help!, I needed HEALING, I wanted a NEW foundation!

Get ready to take a ride with me on my healing journey where I had to face and conquer my trauma head on. I had to revisit the homes of my life journey, to start to dismantle the walls, the hallways, the closet spaces. The interior and exterior of the foundation of each domicile that spoke so many lies, dysfunction, mayhem, trauma and so forth to me. Just like the Halloween franchise, I myself experienced something in my personal and spiritual home that was HAUNTING to my soul.

I had to DEEP clean the Haunted Houses of My life Journey.

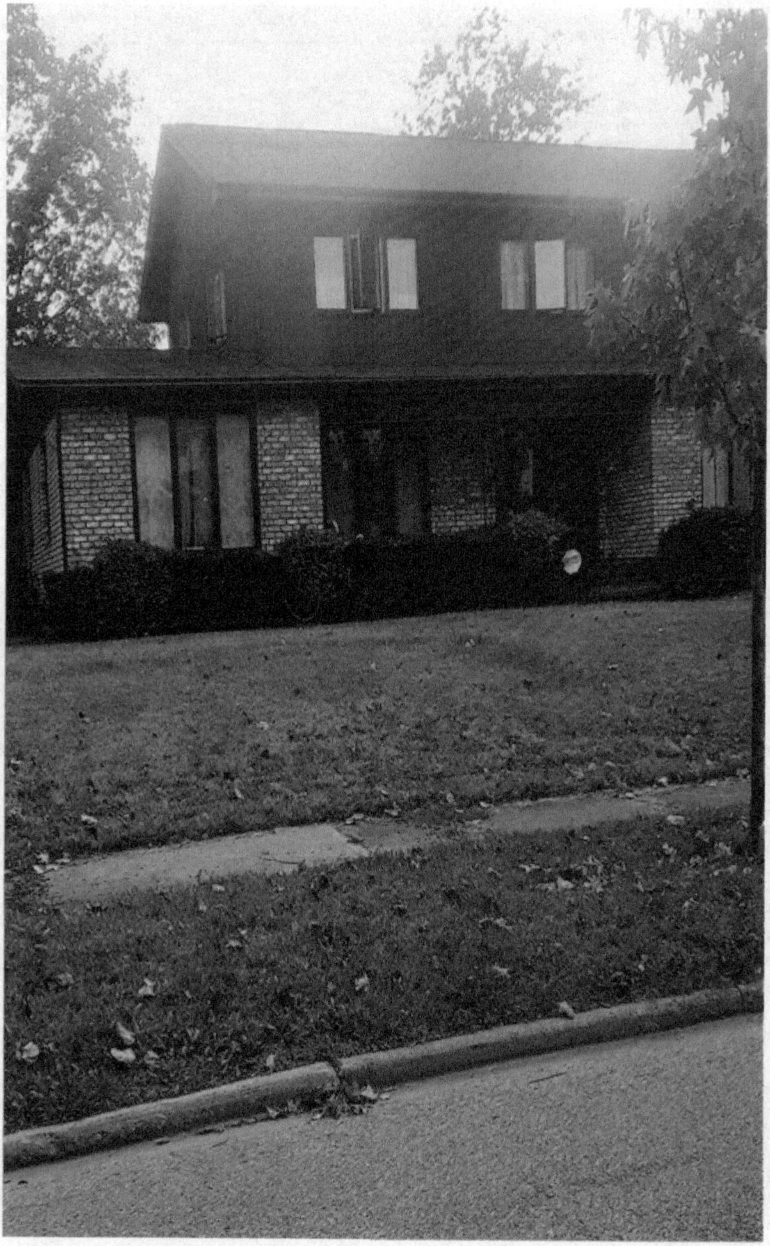

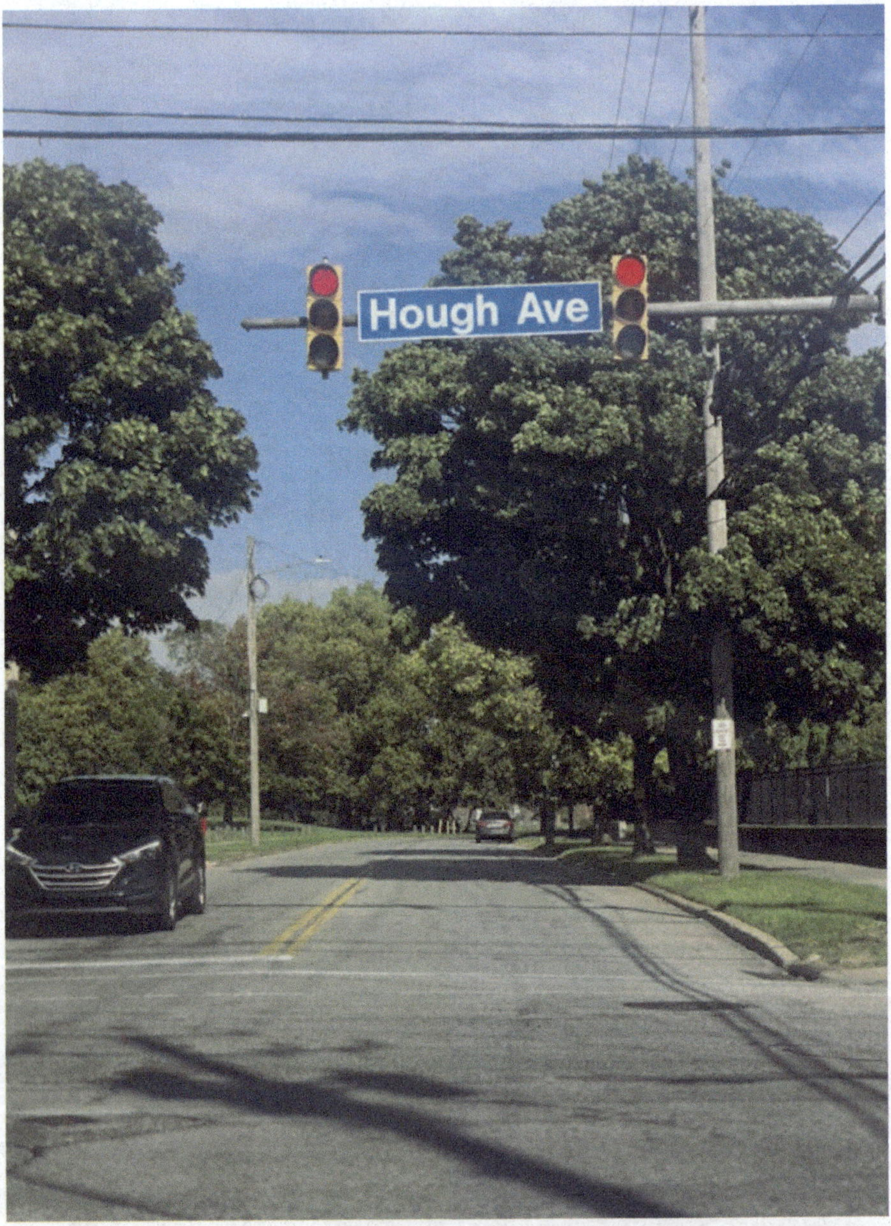
Hough Ave

During a church service, one Sunday I heard two words that changed the trajectory of my healing process in a positive manner. Those words were GENERATIONAL CURSE(s). When I heard those two words something in me ignited, I want to learn more about this Thing called GENERATIONAL CURSE(S). What did this curse entail? Who was cursed? I wanted to know If I was part of a Generational Curse? This sparked my desire to learn more.

What is Generational Curse? It isn't necessarily always NEGATIVE, however, for the most part there are negative understandings and consequences that are associated with the GENERATIONAL CURSE(S) that are connected to one's family lineage (FAMILY TREE) through one's DNA, blood line, ancestry and environment.

Let's get ready to meet The PARENTS, Karen and Thomas.

Mother was from the east side of town, which was the Mt. Pleasant and Kinsman area of Cleveland, Ohio. Considered a very nice area during the time that my mom was growing up (1950-1970 era), mother's household consisted of two parents along with her three other siblings one brother and two sisters, who I simply adored and who had the pleasure of making beautiful memories with. Mother, to my understanding did very well in school. Her academic status was beyond up to par making her a straight A student. She was on the cheer leading squad and captain of the cheer leading team. She also engaged in other extra curriculum programs, which made her popular among the other students and school staff. I really think school, for Mother, was her safe haven. Home away from home. Her Peace places.

Mother's family dynamics and her generational curses were ordained to intertwine with another person. They would combine each other's household traumas together, meshing her pain and disappointments with his. Even though they were from two different sides of town they both shared similar dysfunctions which made many of their home environment experiences together a bit challenging emotionally, spiritually, and physical disarray, just to name a few, but first the Girl had to meet a boy .... THE DAD!

"Sometimes our common connection with another person is our SHARED traumas, which can set up collateral damage to the soul. But! Thanks to God graces and mercy I'm here to tell you that there is Victory and Healing for a soul whose heart is filled with a painful path of destruction, caused by battle wounds of GENERATIONAL CURSES. Victory can be yours, it's definitely MINES...GLORY BE TO GOD!

So now that we have the Girl (Mom) in place, Mother had to start her own journey at a very early age, like I stated earlier, due to some very destructive situations in her home with her parents, which most likely dwelled in her parents' lineage due to the generational curses handed to them.

My mom was forced into becoming self-sufficient around the tender age of 13 years old. I know that was a very challenging time for my mom being that, at this age, her worries consisted of making sure that your homework was done, having fresh and clean clothing, trying to figure her next meal. While those young years should have consisted of my mom trying to cultivate relationships with other children her age, doing what preteens do, like going to the movies, roller skating, things of that nature, yet, she's trying to figure out how to balance going to school and finding a place to lay her head. My heart goes out to my mom for having to endure such heavy and painful circumstances at such an early stage of her life. During the course of her negative and abusive circumstances it definitely damaged her heart in many ways but also made her warrior, Something I absolutely inherited from her. As my mom pushed through finding her footing in this world, she found some comfort in her grandmother, Mother Minnie, who was more of a mother figure to her. She was able to attain some life skills and womanly advice from her Grandmother Minnie, which brought some much needed structure in her life. Grandmother Minnie lived a very long life and gained a lot of wisdom along the way in spite of her own generational circumstances.

Life is getting ready to show up real tough and abrasive as the girl is getting ready to meet the BOY! Dad!

There are layers upon layers of trauma and dysfunction that one has to shed before one can even see a glimmer of hope, peace and joy. Let's keep going. Let's get to the tools needed to clean out those haunted houses so we can live in a Victorious HEALING home.

My Dad was raised on the east side of town, in the Cedar, Hough, 105th areas of Cleveland, Ohio. These areas were way different from the side of town where my mother was raised. Dad's side of town was considered the inner city. There were a lot of movement and people flowing everywhere, let's just say a lot of

HUSTLE going on. There was always something going on at each corner and cross streets on dad's side of town. Lots of activity and entertainment going on, there was never a dull moment on his stomping grounds. IT WAS A LOUD ENVIRONMENT!

Dad had fourteen other siblings. The first set of children (the first seven older children including Dad had a different Father). The last set of siblings had their own dad. I had the pleasure of meeting both Grandfathers. For the most part dad was raised in a single parent home. With a set up like that and not having a strong parental environment in place for him and his fourteen siblings, there was a greater chance that dad and his siblings would lack parental attention and nurturing that a child would want to receive from a parent(s). Let's just say with that volume of children in a home with one parent, I'm quite sure there was constant mayhem and ruckus going in each part of the home. Someone was more prone to get swept under the rug, NOT SEEN! Being deprived of their needs and wants, I'm quite sure some of the older siblings had to play the parent at times, which absolutely brought on some feelings of resentments and grudges towards their parents. These two entities are a type of generational curse that plays in the destruction of family dynamics. Resentment and grudges are damaging to many people's hearts and life path, that prevents them from living THEIR BEST and healthy life.

With those types of environmental challenges and dysfunction, my dad was forced into SURVIVAL MODE at the early of three. Dad had to learn the crossroads and streetlights of the Cleveland streets way too soon, Dad was exploring life through adult eyes and not by choice. My dad should have been exploring life through a child's eyes. Instead of engaging in school activities and simply just being a young child, playing football, riding his bike with other children, my dad was exploring the world as an adult on his terms without any navigational tools from either parent.

We all know that the Streets at times don't quite love you like a parent would. Truthfully, the street life doesn't quite love anyone at times, let alone a little child that was set to be free on his own. The streets became my dad's parents. HE WAS SET UP FOR FAILURE EARLY IN LIFE. Generational curses and dysfunction isn't set up for you to SUCCEED, it wants you to remain in BONDAGE while giving you the illusion that it LOVES you back, LIES!

My dad was known in the streets of Cleveland. Everyone knew Thomas Knox. Being that dad had to navigate through those Cleveland streets at an early age, he was out there learning and seeing some very harsh things. Navigating through the world, in Survival mode will have you doing some things that are not so pleasing to your soul. Imagine a child out in the streets doing what grown adults do to stay fed, to stay clothed, etc....TO SURVIVE PERIOD!

These types of circumstances for my father led to him falling in LOVE with the LOVE OF THE STREET LIFE. His early years without parental guidance unfortunately CONSUMATED THAT LOVE AFFAIR!

Dad embraced every ounce of the street life and the hustle that it had to offer which created his negative desire for money, love, clothing and the so called "finer things of life." Dysfunctional desires grew out of control. The Hustle mentality was embedded in him, eventually leading to him becoming a thief, con artist and yes, a DRUG DEALER! The company that he kept were cut from the same cloth. His hustling endeavors sent him and his counterparts to go exploring outside of the streets of Cleveland, Ohio. Spreading his wings, the across the highways and byways of many cities and states across the world, making him a nationwide known Hustler. Now that he's internationally known, the street life named him 'Lil Shorty' The Cleveland Hustler.

Dad was birthed into a generational curse that kept him in bondage his entire life. The streets of Cleveland held my dad captive with the facade of the STREET LIFE that had no true LOVE for him or for anyone else that fell in love with it. Dad loved that dysfunctional love affair that he was having with the STREET life. It gave him a false sense of power and courage. Dad was true and loyal to the streets, but the streets cheated on him every chance it could. The street life cheated him out of knowing how to Love himself properly nor how to love someone else properly.

If you haven't seen any remnants of what true love looks like or felt like as a child, you miss the expectation of love that should be a positive nurturing feeling from our parents. If the beginnings weren't healthy inside the four walls of one's home and family dynamics, how can you give or show proper, healthy love towards someone else, especially when your home is haunted with so much pain and dysfunctional.... I'm here to tell that its quite challenging.

My mom was on one side of the world dealing with life and all the baggage that she had to regularly carry around with her. The weight was heavy for her to carry. A bag filled with pain, abandonment, self-esteem issues, longing to belong, just to name a few. Let's just say she toted around a lot emotional, mental and physical garbage. My mom was dealing with life without any real parental guidance or nurturing balance around her, she had to find her own ways to unload those bags of garbage...which came with a price. Unloading baggage isn't always an easy task. Sometimes you need help, my mom had NONE. She had to unload it on her own; however, a desire for most women, is to receive help from a MAN!

My Dad was on other side of the world engulfed in the lies and the facade of the street life. The bags my dad was carrying around were full of a false sense of love, abandonment issues, demons that lie dormant within the walls of his home, and a false sense of belonging. He carried them around on a daily basis, without any healthy parental guidance to help him unload some of his mess. My Dad had to learn his way while attempting to dump some of mess along the way…Trust me his process wasn't successful. His bags kept filling up with more mess.

Now let's get ready for Boy to meet girl. When boy meets girl we will see how they combine all their mess and dysfunction and their HAUNTED HOMES.

While my mother was trying to figure out life on one side of town, my dad was on the other side of town navigating through like a rolling stone. What they didn't know or should I say that they weren't prepared for was that God was preparing for their connection, getting ready to align two damaged hearts.

As mom roamed around she made some connections with some people that were from the inner city that would steer and lead her to a road where she would find her boy…MY DAD!

From my understanding, I don't think it was quite love at first sight. My dad was considered a handsome bad boy. I think that she was intrigued by his bad boy persona that came off MYSTERIOUS TO HER. Being that they were from different sides of that tracks also made him more intriguing to my mom. Dad was used to more of let's say saucier, round-the-way type of women that came from the same street life that he engaged in. My mom was a smart, attractive female. Mom had more of a polished persona about herself which made her invite to my dad. Let's just say they were the poster children for when Polar opposites ATTRACT.

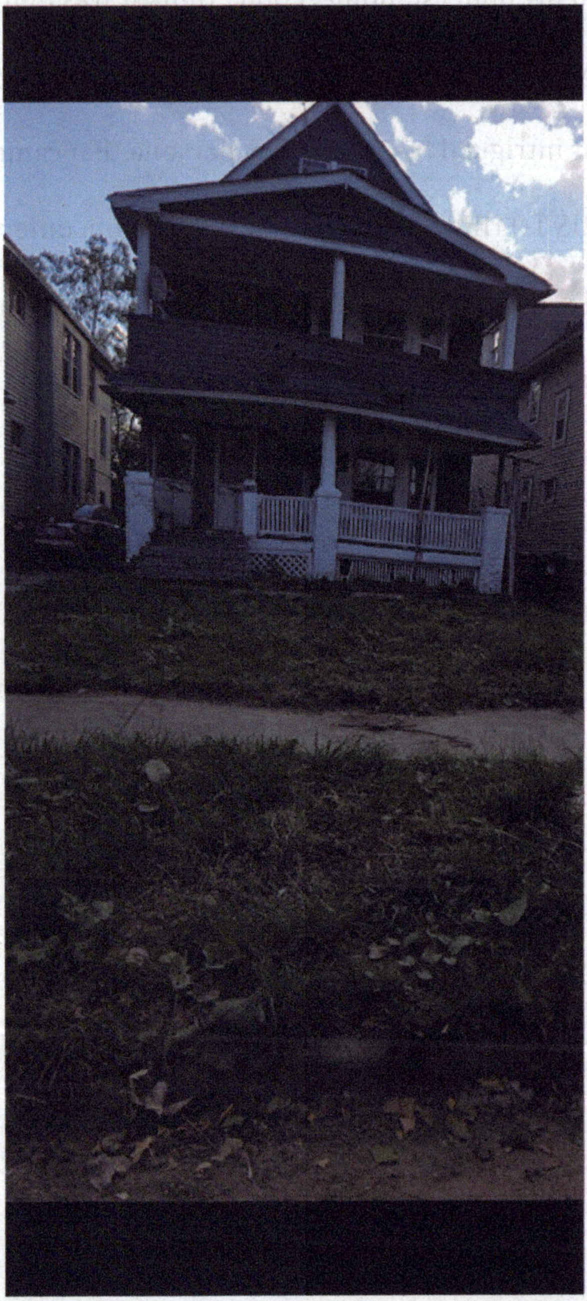

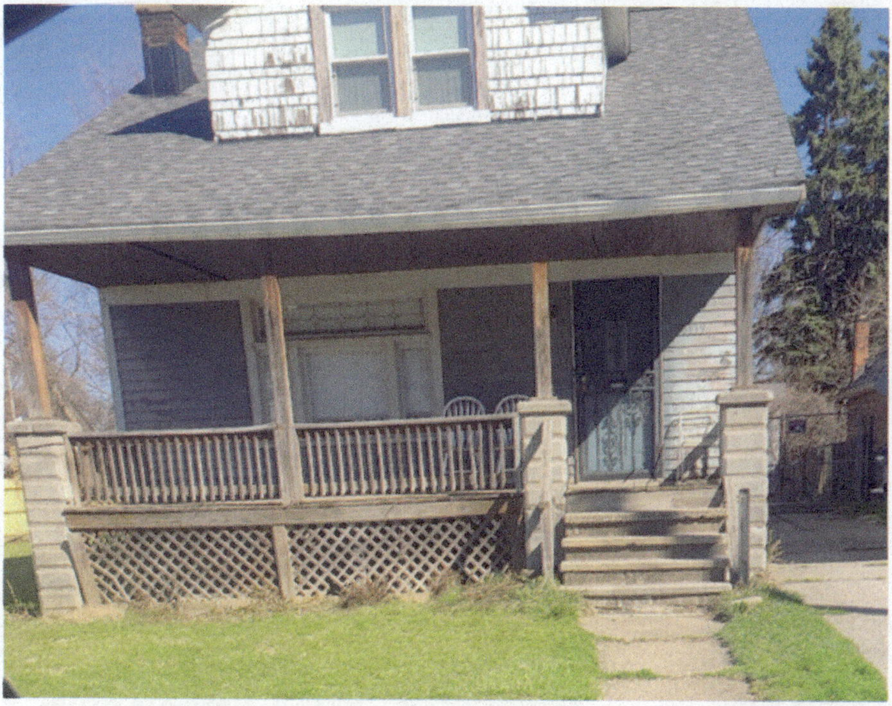

*The Meeting...*

Mother was hanging out at a friend's house who was also friends with one of my dad's sisters who he was living with. The more that my mom hung around her friend's house, the more and more she eventually started engaging in conversations with my dad which led to them hanging out, which led to their LOVE AFFAIR blooming.

For a love connection to bloom and thrive in a healthy manner there should be some things set in place where you need to feel complete with or without another person solidifying your WHOLENESS. Unfortunately, when you're not given those tools to implement that thought process, you're bound to look for completion...WHOLENESS within someone else and if their foundation of SELF is filled with EMPTINESS and PAIN, that Love connection is bound for a lot of PAINFUL and negative dismantling of the MIND, BODY, and SOUL...

My parents' love affair was setup for a lot of FAILURE and HEARTACHE, due to the lack of WHOLENESS within THEMSELVES.

My parents' beginning started off very rocky. We have two damaged hearts, two people from opposite sides of the tracks. Both their homes were haunted by a lot of PAIN and dysfunction and here they are getting ready to mesh both THEIR HAUNTED HOMES TOGETHER.

Even though my parents' commonality was filled with some of the same generational curses, my mother's life path had a little more positive groundings for her being that she was smart and attractive. Her career endeavors were set up for many positive successful choices. She had more career options, whereas my dad was for the streets and being gainfully employed wasn't in the cards for him. Since mom choose to be connected to a person that wasn't quite be able to be a provider for her on a consistent basis. There are seasons that came with the street life. One season you were your sitting on top of the world in the FACADE of GRANDEUR. Money is rolling in left and right. Then there's the seasons where things are slow and running dry and you didn't know where your next dollar was coming from. These are the dynamics that came with my dad which brought on a lot of strife to my mom's family. My dad's lifestyles were very frowned upon by my mother's parents which made the courtship very challenging...Another setup for failure in my parents LOVE CONNECTION.

Now, to add fuel to the fire during the cultivation of the haunted houses that my parents were preparing, my parents are bringing a child into the world that will share their haunted path with them. That child would be ME!

My being born into this world wasn't quite a pleasant or joyful beginning, being that my parents weren't married yet and being that she was underage. My grandparents placed my mom in an all-girl facility for under aged pregnant girls (those were things that did back then, or you would go secretly live with other family members until you gave birth). My grandparents were not too ecstatic with the fact my mother was getting ready to have a child with my dad. Like I stated, my grandparents weren't quite a fan of my dad, his lifestyle and his upbringing. And now, my parents are getting ready to add a baby to their house of dysfunction. HAUNTED HOUSES don't quite care how many people dwell in the domicile of PAIN, CHAOS, ABUSE. These are just a few things that lie dormant within the walls of the HAUNTED HOUSE, as long as they can continue to HAUNT your soul while keeping you lost and trapped inside.

The Birthing of ME and the Labor Pains that came with it caused a lot of strife and Chaos between my parents' homes.

May 21,1968, my born date. I was born TRACY S. SADDLER (UNTIL FURTHER NOTICE) Being that my parents were not married, there were some legal issues with the courts system of Cleveland, Ohio that had to take place between both sides of my family. My dad wasn't quite pleased with the fact that I did not carry his last name...KNOX!

Let the battle begin...

Now the courts were involved in the proceeding of SADDLER vs KNOX. To my understanding these were trying times for both sides of my family. My dad would catch the bus on every court date to fight for his baby girl, the right to have her name changed. I was told when the judge would announce in the case of TRACY S. SADDLER vs Thomas Knox, he would lose his cool. He was held in contempt of court at many of the hearings. When the courts kept announcing my last name as SADDLER, my dad felt like I was being called a BASTARD CHILD which did not sit well with him AT ALL By the time of their last court date my parents had eloped (snuck and got married) in Detroit; therefore, the Cleveland courts system granted my name changed to…TRACY S. KNOX.

My early beginnings were a battle and I had been fighting to fit in ever since…I fight no more! Now that my name change was established there was a little more harmony developing between the two family's despite of the arguing and fight that took place before and after my birth. My parents and my mother's parents, more so, decided to put their differences aside to help in the care of providing for me.

My parents settled on the east side in the Hough and Cedar areas of Cleveland, my dad's stomping grounds. We resided in a one-bedroom apartment. I remember my mother would try to make our home as cozy as possible. She held down a job while my dad ran the streets. She would obtain credit at different stores to furnish our home (just like rental centers of today). Whatever we may have been going through, she gave her best efforts, in making our home feel comfortable instead of gloomy or sad. Something I emulate from her (remember what I said about you getting pieces and parts of you from your parents, even if you knew them or not). Then it happened...

I noticed that my dad wasn't around. He wasn't there for our morning routine of waking me up for school and prepping my breakfast, as I watched cartoons (Back in the day my favorite cartoon was Bugs Bunny and his crew). Then off to Charles Orr Elementary school we went. Ut was not far from our apartment so we would walk. Our daily routine was off, dad wasn't there! Several days had passed. Days turned into weeks, then months, then I heard the word JAIL!?(a word that still haunts me to this day). My dad was arrested and confined to jail for engaging in some his street life endeavors. This was a sad and empty time of my childhood life. Our little cozy home became haunted with sadness and emptiness, I could see the disappointment and sadness in my mother's eyes. In spite of it all, she tried her best, to provide, keep me together and stay on our daily routine without my dad being there.

He's Back!!

After a couple months after being in county jail, Dad walked through the doors of our home, as if he had never left. I was super excited that he had returned to us. Just as before, we fell right back into our daily routine. Although he was back home, I was haunted with these strange feelings and emotions. Nervousness set in. I would always wonder if he would be home when I get back from school. Is he back in jail? Him leaving at the time developed some trauma for me, I felt abandoned...Abandonment is an entity that loves to flow through cracks and crevices in the walls of many HAUNTED HOMES'. Trauma doesn't care where it RESIDES. It just wants to torment and haunt every essence of your core and soul.

When your soul is haunted by different negative experiences, it keeps you IMPRISONED and trapped in those GENERATIONAL CURSES within the walls of your personal and spiritual homes, keeping you from living your best and healed LIFE.

My mother felt that it was time to leave the side of town where my dad was from and move closer to her side of town. My dad's stomping grounds were becoming too loud and too busy for mom's liking, she wanted to reside on the other side where she was from. The Hustle and Bustle of the streets, she thought, was a little calmer and more peaceful. So, she thought!

My Grandparents were building a house in the suburbs of Shaker Hts, Ohio. My mom accepted my grandfather's offer for us to move into the home that were moving out of. We started our new journey, in a new neighborhood that was a little more pleasant than the neighborhood we left. I loved our new neighborhood. I quickly made new friends being that I often visited when my grandparents were still living there. I absolutely enjoyed being around my new friends. We would explore and go on many adventures through the neighborhood. We rode our bikes all around the streets. Played outdoor games like "Hide-And-Go-Seek". I was free to do all the things a child should be engaging in. My dad played a huge part in making sure that I experienced all the fun things that life had to offer a child and the positive experience that came along with it. We did everything. We went to amusement parks, golfing (I loved to drive the golf carts). We played tennis at the park, went swimming on a regular at Woodhill Park, The fun part about these outings is that my dad took my friends along, the more the merrier for me. Those feelings of him leaving unexpectedly began to subside just a little.

I was now in a new neighborhood full of friends and family. My mother added another playmate to the equation when she gave birth to my little sister. Joy was spurring out all over the place.

Things were going very well for a while within the walls of our new place, our home did not seem as haunted and empty. There were a lot of awesome memories developing within the hallways and walls of our new home. My childhood journey felt pretty peaceful and pleasant for a long time. I was finally able to experience some wonderful childhood moments.

Let the Shenanigans Begin…

Misery loves company. She loves to show up unexpectedly just to remind you of her miserable ass. Slowly but surely Misery found herself creeping back into our home with the intent of disturbing and haunting the peaceful foundation that we were trying to build in our lives. My mother's upbringing in a structured yet emotionally strained environment and my father's chaotic, street-influenced childhood both contributed to my foundation.

Dysfunction NEVER wants us to REST IN PEACE. It wants to steal, kill and destroy any type of PEACE that you accumulated and carried along the way. Dysfunction despises HAPPINESS. One of the things traumas feed off of is chaos and boy was chaos brewing everywhere in our lives.

My parents were trying their best to live in a positive functioning way, but with dysfunction illuminating from both sides of the family, it brought on some very challenging and abrasive moments between the two families. It started becoming volatile.

The battle between families started to affect my parents' marriage SEVERELY! It was like the HATFIELDS vs The McCoy's, one the most known family feuds of all times.

The battle began because my dads family felt like my mom was trying to take my father away from them. Although my dad's finances came from the streets, to his family he was the BREADWINNER. It didn't matter if the money came from legal or illegal endeavors, my dad's family felt like my mother was stepping on their toes when it came to how my dad was distributing his funds. My mom didn't play about how she took care of my sister and I or how she ran her home, so fiances became a big issue between the families. Everyone wanted a piece of my dad's STREET PIE.

Other negative dynamics added to the family chaos of division including my dad's family labeling my mother as BEING BOUJEE! They felt like she was acting as if she better than them.

They felt like she thought she was cut from better cloth than they were. The crazy part is, BOTH SIDES OF MY FAMILY, were ALL cut from the same CLOTH of DYSFUNCTION.... see that's one of the TRICKS of dysfunction and trauma. It tries to DRESS you up in layers of DECEIT and DELUSION, making you think that just because you wear your DYSFUNCTION and trauma differently there's NO WAY that you are cut from same DYSFUNCTIONAL cloth that others wear. IT'S ALL LIES! It's all a ploy; a trick to keep you stuck in that HAUNTED HOUSE of TRAUMA and DYSFUNCTION keeping you from facing and healing from those Generational Curses that Haunt your life's journey daily.

    Those battles between the families took me on an emotional roller coaster. The fighting and arguing was more than a notion. My parents were fighting more and more. The division between the families was badly haunting our home. It was all taking a mental toll on me. I started developing real bad anxiety, I was nervous about what was next. The physical fighting was making my body very anxious, overwhelming thoughts haunted my mind and body. I wanted to escape from in between the haunted walls of my home. My home started to be plagued with violence and heartache. GOD, DO YOU SEE THIS!? GOD HELP US! GOD, WE NEED YOU! Those were the words that roamed through my spirit on a constant basis. GOD HELP ME!

I was seeing violence, heartache, and division at a rapid rate throughout my family dynamics. I would escape into my world of TELEVISION & MUSIC. I needed an outlet of escape so that I would NOT see and feel the horrors of my life. Television allowed me to envision what a good family life appeared to be through the families on T.V. Back then we had all types of family T.V. shows: the Brady Bunch, the Partridge Family, the Cosby show, all displaying something that I craved for, a UNITED FAMILY LIFE, even in the midst of their adversity those families seemed to find a healthy way to figure their problems out. There was more laughter and joy that seeped out every room of their home. I would envision being one characters on those shows. It didn't matter if they were black or white characters, I just wanted to be anybody but ME!

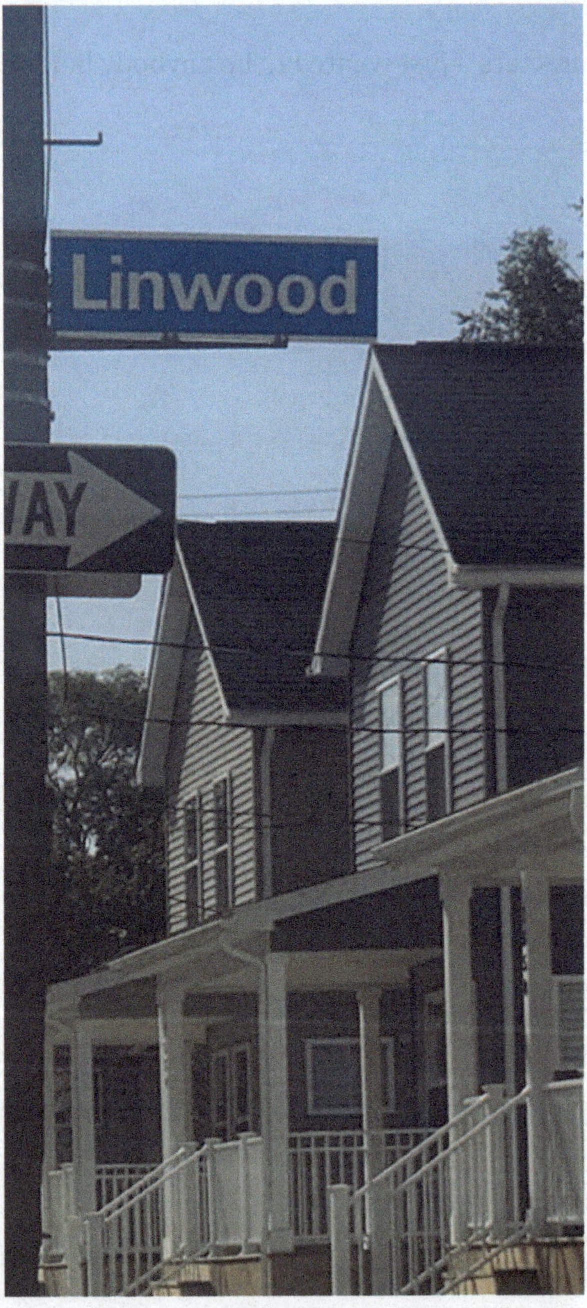
Linwood

My escape into the SOUND of MUSIC took my mind off the chaos that ran deep in my soul. The LYRICS to certain songs were like paint to me. I would take certain lyrics from different songs and PAINT on a PLAIN CANVAS creating the WORLD that I desired, full of bright colors and flowers. DARK COLORS were NOT allowed on my MUSICAL CANVAS. I wanted to see NOTHING but BRIGHT COLORS, to me they equated to JOY. Painting those LYRICAL words to music would allow me to escape into my PEACE of MIND world where I could smile and laugh. THE LOVE OF MUSIC I felt it LOVED ME back.

WHEN I ESCAPED I HAD A CHANCE TO CREATE MY OWN FAMILY DYNAMICS...THAT WERE FILLED WITH LOTS OF LOVE and NO DYSFUNCTION!The reality of my life always reminded me that my escape into that fantasy was so far from the TRUTH of my life.

REALITY -Vs- FANTASY...

After the music stopped playing and my television shows went off, the fantasies that took me away for a moment, MY TEMPORARY RELIEF, I had to come off that high of temporary RELIEF and come back to MY REAL-LIFE REALITY. I opened my eyes to see that things were still the painful SAMB! Still Haunted with sadness.

GOD WHERE ARE YOU!!

In between the good and bad moments of my life I began to feel a presence that was starting to CHASE me. It was an ugly dark presence showing up in my sleep. Showing up in dreams trying haunt my soul. Nothing about this entity was pleasant. Whatever it was it knew how to feed off of the NEGATIVITY that haunted through lies dormant in the walls of other homes!

GOD WHERE ARE YOU!

I always knew in my soul that there was something GREATER than me. Something or someone that brought a PRESENCE of LOVE around. No one told me about a GOD/God. It was a KNOWING that always traveled near me. I COULD FEEL IT! But that ugly demonic entity DID NOT WANT ME TO KNOW IT!. I had more life to LIVE, to connect to it. Until then I had fought through this haunted house that was tormenting my SPIRITUAL and PERSONAL domain.

See, sometimes when the dysfunction is on a continual HAUNT to destroy you, it will follow you from HOUSE to HOUSE.

Ten years have now passed since we moved into my grandparents' home and by this time, I had seen it ALL! Fights on top of fights once I even saw a shootout between the two families. YES! A Shoot Out! My Nervous system was paying the price from this chaos. I was always on pins and needles, trying to protect my little sister from it. GOD DO YOU SEE THIS MESS. HELP!

My parents were going through these on and off breaks up that affected me something awful. My anxieties were spurring out of control. there would be moments after the vicious fights, she'd throw my dad out in the middle of the night, and I would have to go with him. Him and I would walk in the middle of the night, NO CAR! to his Mother's house. You are talking about DEVASTATED! Not only was I haunted by ABANDONMENT now I'm haunted by REJECTION!

In my child-minded head I'm going... GOD WHAT DID I DO!!???! As we walked over to a place where nothing, but DEMONS ROAMED THROUGH the entire house! The place where MOLESTATION, ALCOHOL, DRUGS and PARENTAL SUPERVISION haunted every nook and cranny of the walls! GOD WHY DID SHE PUT ME OUT!? Dad would leave me there and go on his merry war! WHY ARE YOU LEAVING ME AGAIN!?

Thank God the next day my mother would come and get me, but that still didn't take away the fact that she put me OUT with Him. WHY MOTHER!? What did I do to deserve that? was something that I always wanted to ask. As a child I could NOT! So I stayed in bondage wrapped in abandonment and rejection issues that would follow me through my life's journey.

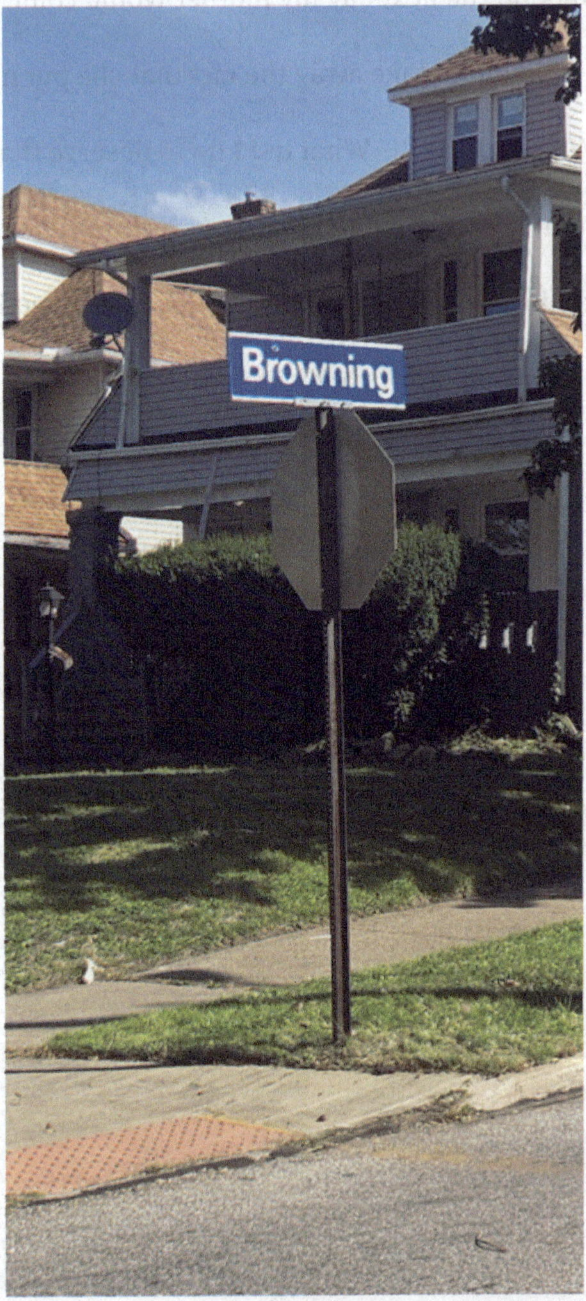
Browning

DEATH!

Like I stated, ten years had passed, and death started to show up in my family. When my Grandmother Susan, my dad's mother passed away, the chaos and division was at a level ten. The fighting between each of his sibling over material things that my grandmother had obtained through the years, such as her home. She wasn't even in the ground yet and here they are battling over who gets what!

My parents came together and decided to let them have it ALL! Together my parents made an executive decision to part ways with his side of the family and step away from the chaos for a while, which was much needed for my soul.

# ON TO THE NEXT!

Not only did we step away for a while, my family and I moved to another neighborhood. We moved near my mother's parents in the suburbs of Shaker Heights, Ohio. I was already familiar with that area, being that my grandparents were living there. I was already acclimated to the surrounding area of Shaker Heights. When I found out that we were moving there I was ecstatic. I always enjoyed that area. It was surrounded by so much greenery, beautiful trees, and flowers everywhere. My grandparents had a big, beautiful home with a lot of land to roam through. In between the chaos and dysfunction of life, I enjoyed going over there. It was a place where I could escape and pretend that their homes were my own personal mansion. I could pretend that my husband and children were living lavishly in our own joyful and pleasant domicile. There were so many rooms and so much space to explore at my grandparents' house in Shaker Heights. Those moments over there is where my soul felt quiet and at ease for once... The chaos and dysfunction at my grandparents' home WASN'T AS LOUD over there...remember dysfunctions come in different unhealthy functions. It is loud or quiet at times, either way it still equals DYSFUNCTION.

New Beginnings... but the same chaos is waiting around the corner.

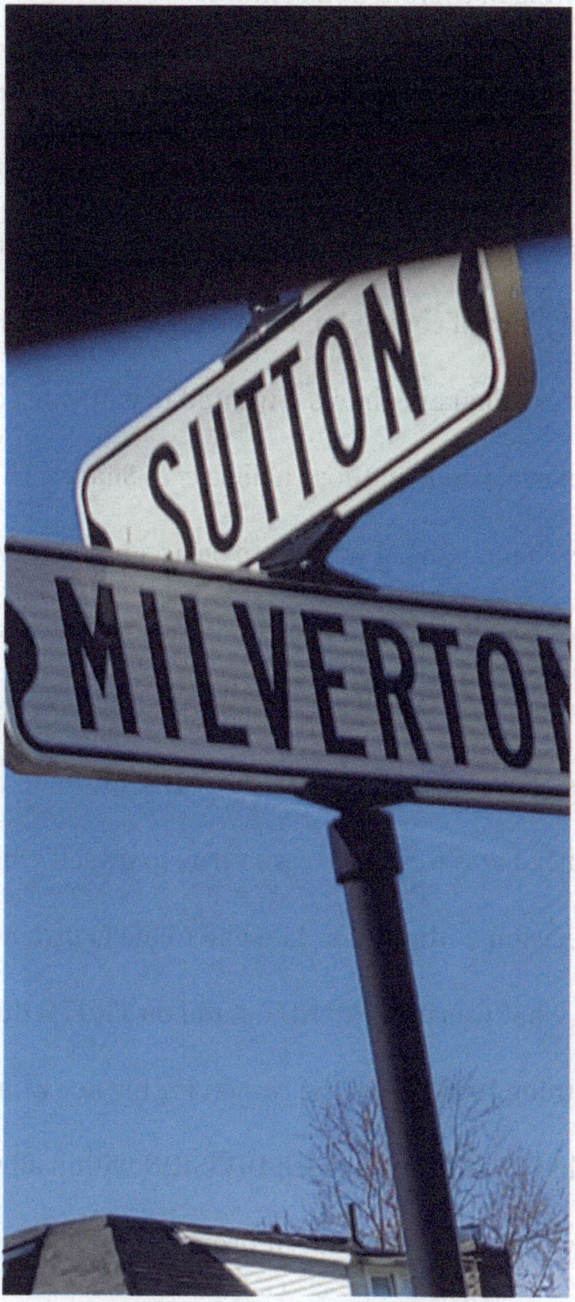
SUTTON
MILVERTON

Let the haunting of dysfunction continue.

So here we are in our new place, new surroundings, and hopefully new beginnings. The first couple years living in Shaker was as normal as could be. The norm of many new friends is always uneasy, but of course I made friends within the hallways and corridors of Shaker Schools. I wanted to cultivate connections with some of everybody in those hallways at Shaker. The balance at times was challenging. I wanted to be accepted by everyone but there was the pressure of choosing sides or which crew you wanted to hang with. We all know POPULARTITY reeks through the hallways of every school, so if I chose the so-called popular crew of Shaker, I was torn and wasn't true to myself when I made the decision at that time. Life had to life in order for me to understand what was in me to NOT stand on TRUTH during those times. One thing I did know; the reason for my not wanting to pick sides, was that I had seen so much DIVISION within all sides of my families. If you didn't pick a side, it brought on a lot of confusion and strife between each other. These are some of the things that HAUNTED souls experience. Different types of dysfunctions will show in your life. Dysfunction will have you choosing UNHEALTHY people, places, and things. Dysfunction loves to see you trying to be VALIDATED by UNHEALTHY entities that meant me you absolutely no good. This created a whole life filled with TRAUMA BONDING.

When you learn better...You will DO BETTER...FORGIVE YOURSELF!

Trauma and dysfunction are always LURKING around the corner ready to pop out any given moment, ready to HAUNT you once again with its shenanigans and boy was it lurking its ugly presence around my corners.

Here we go AGAIN!..

For a while things were pretty quiet at home. Life was doing its usual things. My mom was maintaining the house, supervising my sister and I. My mother always held down some type job and dad was still participating in his street life endeavors.

    The walls of our home were starting to rattle with some familiar noises. The ghosts of dysfunction were trying to creep out through the open crevices of each room of our home. My parents started having some small arguments, the normal arguments couples have during their relationship. Eventually their arguments slowly led to some huge fights. My body was starting to be infiltrated with some very haunted, familiar feelings. Nervousness was starting to inflame my soul. I started mumbling HERE WE GO AGAIN!...The fear of my mom putting me out with my dad was escalating in my spirit and eventually it happened!..She put my dad out again, surprisingly, this time I was able to stay. I was shocked and for a moment elated I was not put out with him. That feeling of relief was short lived. Trust me when I say that I had to pay the price for being able to stay home. Whatever pain and strife my parents were going through, those temporary separations hit my mothers mind. I reaped the consequences and repercussions of her hurt feelings caused by my dad. It felt like the mere presence of me, reminded my mom of my dad in more ways than one. Every chance she got her demeanor and her harsh words towards me let me know that I was a constant reminder of him.

HURT PEOPLE HURT PEOPLE.

I always played the middleman between my parents disconnection, meaning that when it came to the communication between each other, my mother would use me to reach out to my dad when we were in need of financial assistance for the household. I hated to be the go between my parents and their mess, I ABSOLUTELY DESPISED IT! GOD WHERE ARE YOU!...I DON'T WANT TO BE PART OF THEIR HURT and CHAOS!...HELP ME!

The cycle of their madness would sometimes go on for months at a time. My dad would either return on his own or there were moments when my mom would pack my sister and I up and we set out on a journey to find him. Sometimes we would go as far as Toronto, Canada to find him, which was one of the places he could utilize some illegal skills as part of his HUSTLE. Oh yes! Dysfunction will have you on the roads of despair and false hope,trying to return you back to that TRAUMA BOND connection that keeps you in the cycle of damn near INSANITY, WHERE YOU KEEP GETTING THE SAME NEGATIVE RESULTS TO A SITUATION that has no real POSITIVE RESOLUTION and you're on the brink of EMOTIONAL, PHYSICAL, MENTAL BREAK DOWN!.

See we tend to return to certain situations, that majority of the time aren't HEALTHY for us. We tend to return HOPING each time that the situation will get better. Nine times of ten IT DOESN'T pan out that way and here you are right back in line, boarding the ROLLERCOASTER ride of DYSFUNCTION, that lands you back into the arms of TRAUMA and CHAOS...TRAUMA BONDING is a repeated cycle of trauma which is also a friend of Codependency.

We make many excuses to keep from entertaining the GHOST OF DYSFUNCTION, you know the ones. I have to stay for the kids to keep the family together. They need me. It will get better. They're just going through something. And the all time favorite.. BUT! I LOVE THEM...Trust me the list goes on. We all have dealt with the LIST at one point or another. It's ok..FORGIVE YOURSELF!.

When I say that I was constantly praying for peace for a home that was plagued by so much turmoil and pain. I had to ACT LIKE everything was peachy keen in our HAUNTED HOUSE, because the worst part was that the people thought that because my sister and I came from a two parent home, lived in the suburbs and we had things, through their eyes the foundation of our home appeared solid, and behind the windows of our home there was no way strife and dysfunction lived there. BOY! Were they wrong!.

Facade is one of the tricks of dysfunction. It gives you the illusion that everything is OKAY, that from what others see, the exterior foundation of you, gives the appearance that you are functioning in a positive, healthy manner, meanwhile, what they truly don't see is that your interior is being tormented by pain and so much more. So therefore due to what everyone thought my life was behind those closed doors, I went along with it and I carried around the Facade that everything on my home front, was okay.

Needless to say what they didn't know is that I was dying inside those four walls! I use my comedic nature to mask the pain I was dealing with within my haunted home of HURT!.

You are talking about the TEARS OF CLOWN! I was the poster child for that statement. Many, many days and nights after making the world laugh and seeming to bubble to the world...I would cry my soul to sleep!

I HATE YOU TRAUMA!..You're robbing my peace and my JOY!

We spent over fifteen years living in Shakers Heights, we actually lived in two homes in Shaker. There were some seasons in those fifteen years where the four walls of my homes would whisper little bouts of dysfunction enough to have some remnants of some peaceful moments.

After graduating from Shaker Heights High school, I was preparing to leave for college, I was headed to Kent State University in Portage County,Ohio. Kent State University will always have special place in my heart. My Kent State days allowed me to be away from those hard moments back at home. I felt free while attending Kent State. I met some awesome people with whom I was able to make special connections with. We are still friends to this day. God was showing me that there are some good people out there in this world. My time on the yard gave me a snippet of what PEACE felt like. Kent State University was one reason I wanted to continue my quest to find peace in my life. Kent state made feel FREE FOR A MOMENT!.

When you get a snippet of what peace feels like you will desire it more and more. You'll start chasing it like a drug, wanting to get addicted to the very essence of it, but life had to life some more.

BUCKLE UP MY TRACY...GOD WHERE ARE YOU TAKING ME!?

God was preparing a love for me that I couldn't even fathom its experience ..

I was back home from Kent State for about three years. I returned with much anxiety at having to enter back into a home that I tried escape from, to break free from pain that I was experiencing inside. Soon as I walked through those doors, those haunted walls were more than excited to greet me with its foolery. Here I am facing another crossroads of life, trying to figure out my next move. Back home I rekindle with some old friends from school, that were out in street life, straight on survival mode. See, by the time I returned home, the Cleveland streets I once knew were singing a different tune from when I left for college.

The Cleveland Streets were singing LOUDLY. There were people moving around everywhere! Cars were spinning with loud colors, big gold and silver shiny tires were spinning out of control at every street light and stop sign for you to admire their vehicles, loud music was blasting through every window of every car, every corner had something going on filled with busyness and different types of exchanges between each other. The clothing that everyone was wearing made some type of loud statement, the loud colors, the extreme hairstyles...My, My!

GOD WHAT DID I COME HOME TO!!!?!..

I came back home to the DOPE SCENE...

The people that I was hanging with were enjoying every ounce of the LOUD and RAPID movement of those Cleveland streets. We started going to nightclubs on the west and east side of Cleveland, when I say the streets were bumping morning, noon and night, it seemed as if no one ever slept. The more I hung out around my friends, the more the STREET LIFE was calling my name and boy was it calling my name LOUDLY!,

Then it happened...I answered the CALL of The STREET LIFE!.

Watching others being on straight survival mode getting their needs met by any means necessary and possible, the dope scene was a different type of dysfunction. That dysfunction definitely didn't care who it recruited.

My crew was getting money by the dope boys, (that wasn't quite my forte). To keep up with dope scene you must look the part, if the financing wasn't coming in from the dope boys, my crew and I found others ways to get what we needed to look the part for the street, We starting hitting the malls and shopping centers up, to get what we needed to look PLEASING to the street life. We started stealing our attire, the first time that I ever stole anything, I was nervous as hell, bubble guts, sweating the whole nervous nine yard, my first try was not successful I only came out with one pair of shorts, but I came out feeling like I was the shit... THE FALSE GRANDEUR... is one of the tricks of the ENEMY!.

The more I engaged in taking clothes from the stores, the more I gained a false sense of power... I eventually strayed away from the crowd when I went on my stealing sprees. I figured that the crowd was drawing too much attention to us, so I started going alone. My street mind was DEVELOPING!

Once I ventured off on my own, I had an idea to start selling the items to local establishments around the city of Cleveland. I monopolized a few beauty shops, barber shops and so forth...YOU COULD NOT TELL ME NOTHING!..

I had transformed into a full-Fledged BOOSTER...The birthing of An illegal Clothing Sales person...

My dad's street life DNA was running through my veins...

God Hold My hands ....Take me away from This!.

I was engaged in street life for about two years and like the saying everything must come to an end... EVERYTHING HAS AN EXPIRATION DATE.

Watch what you pray for. God will answer your prayer his way and that's exactly what he did. My Love Affair with the Street Life ended abruptly when I heard the words, STOP! Let me see what's in that bag!?...The police came and broke me and my clothing love affair up. That false power was diminished within two point three seconds, IT WAS OVER!...A weekend in jail (twice) was enough to taint my desire for the street life and if that wasn't enough I had to face the consequences and repercussions of my actions.

I had to face my Illegal charges in court...

GUILTY!....PROBATION!..IF I SEE YOU IN HERE AGAIN!...I'M GOING TO MAKE AN EXAMPLE OUT OF YOU!

Judge, you don't have to worry about ME!....THIS RELATIONSHIP IS OVER!

Wait! What's this feeling that I'm feeling God!?...God, I'm feeling Sick!

Tracy I told you to buckle up, I have something birthing inside of you!

Before my court date I notice some changes in my body, I wasn't too well for a couple of weeks, I thought it was a cold that I couldn't quite shake. My hairdresser noticed that I wasn't feeling well and she said some words that shook me to core and place into straight denial, those words were...

YOU MAY BE PREGNANT!...

Nawl! Not me!...I'm Not ready for that!... My life isn't ready for that!

GOD IS THIS TRUE!....A BABY!?

God what are you Preparing For Me!?.

When my hairdresser uttered those words to me, I continued to brush it off as a cold or the flu. I made a doctor's appointment to see what was going on with me. The day of my doctor's appointment I just figured that the doctor would examine me, give me some medicine and send me on my merry way. The exam was over and I waited patiently for the nurse to return and give me my prescription(s).

The nurse returned, I reached out my hand to receive the script for my medication and she said to me, "Miss Knox, I would like to say that your test came back POSITIVE! THAT YOU ARE PREGNANT!"

The world stood still for what seemed like hours, I said WHAT!?

She said that you are pregnant and she asked, "Are you ok!." I said Yes!

The nurse said "So what are you going to do, Miss Knox?"

Before I knew it...I said as I stared off in a blank zone..I mumbled..I'M KEEPING IT!..(It was like a KNOWING that I was keeping it, that I couldn't even explain)

The Nurse said good!, You will be just fine, said her congratulations and handed me a prescription for prenatal vitamins.

That was the longest ride home. That ride seemed like it took hours. I was in and out of my emotions, my mind was racing so fast, all I could do was mumble over and over …I'M HAVING A BABY!?...my body, my soul and mind just felt so numb!

God was preparing a blessing for me that I wasn't quite ready for, but there was no turning back, I refused to run from it. I had to face this decision to keep my child head on.

I informed my boyfriend of my decision to keep my child, his response was, YOU'RE PREGNANT TOO!? Letting me know that there was a possibility that he fathered another child. That moment right there was setting the scene for what lied ahead as far as what was going to be expected from him. Next I had to inform my parents; once I got that out of the way, I began my pregnancy process.

The Whispers of my dysfunction…

Dysfunction loves to whisper and remind you of its ugliness. Midway into my pregnancy dysfunction started whispering in my ears things like… LOOK AT YOU BRINGING A BABY INTO THIS MESS!… YOU'RE NOT READY TO LOVE ON A BABY! You don't even love yourself. When I tell you the lies that dysfunctions was whispering to me was absolutely ugly, but I refused to succumb to the ghostly lies of dysfunction, generational curses and trauma.

I started taking my pregnancy seriously, making sure that while my baby was preparing for its entrance into the world, that my mind and body consumed as much peace around me as I possible so that my baby would enter into the world as peaceful as it could. During those months I didn't care what my boyfriend was doing in the streets. I didn't want to be engaged in none of his shenanigans with other females. I sat in peace as much as I could. My focus was on the health of my baby. I shut out the ghostly noises of dysfunction that lies dormant in between the four walls of my home. My Focus was the birth of my child.

April 10th 1993 my beautiful baby boy arrived, baby Tyrese made his way into the world.

Seeing him made me breathe differently. My sweet baby boy, Tyrese, changed the way my heart pulsated.

Then reality started to set in.

GOD, WHAT HAVE I DONE!?..I brought another human being into a world that was full of hurt, pain and disappointments.

GOD WHAT HAVE I DONE!?...My home is filled with a lot of hurt, pain and disappointments.

GOD MY BABY AND I NEED YOU!

Although I had my village when it came to raising Tyrese, there were still a lot of challenges that transpired. Not only was Tyrese the first grandchild for my parents, he was the first grandchild for his dad's parents as well. Remember, I told you when you're in a relationship with someone, you're meshing all of your stuff together. Meshing together the good and the bad of both sides and sometimes the bad out weight the good.

We all know that there is no manual, on how to properly raise a child, given to you when discharged from the hospital, so I did the best I could to nurture, to love Tyrese and provide for him.

By the time Tyrese was two years old, his dad and I went our separate ways. There were too many painful moments dealing with Tyrese's dad. Lets just say that Tyrese's dad was too young for certain responsibility and he was sowing his wild oats to "get it out of his system." For some women we are forced to grow up a little faster than the father. That's exactly what I did.

So the reality of my fantasy was that I be would be raising my child outside of being in a two-parent partnership with Tyrese's dad...GOD ALWAYS HAVE OTHER PLANS FOR YOU. When one doors closes, the other one opens. So I had to step through the exit in order to find out what was on the other side.

By the time Tyrese was three years old I started my quest to MAKE A HEALTHY FUNCTIONING home of our own. I wanted to leave behind any remnants of the haunted dysfunction that I was dwelling in with my parents and sister, and I did just that. It wasn't easy. I made a lot sacrifices, worked many hours doing, many things. In spite of some challenging moments with my village, I'm very grateful for the love and support given to Tyrese and me.

I HAD TO TAKE MY POWER BACK...

I HAD TO PUT ON MY BIG GIRL PANTS..

I needed to stay on my quest to find my PEACE within my own four walls...

Eleven years passed. It was just Tyrese and me. I set out to create a sanctuary of PEACE in our own home. It wasn't an overnight process but with perseverance and determination I made it happen for Tyrese and for myself...when you get a piece of what peace feels like you'll want to chase it even more.

To get your victorious turn around from those things plaguing your soul with so much trauma and dysfunction, you MUST continue to stay the course. The road will be filled with a lot of turbulent seasons on your life's journey. Some days you will most definitely want to abort the course while on your mission to find a happy balance and some type of peace of mind. God NEVER said that every season of your life would be EASY!. But if we seek him, he would hold our hands and guide us to our victorious destination. Remember when I stated that my desire was to REST IN PEACE, while I was still earth? That's exactly what I sought out to do.

Life had to life some more for me. It was like God had placed me in boot camp, preparing and conditioning me for seasons of my life that was meant to damage me, but his true plan was to show me his Love, Grace & Mercy over my life.

STAY BUCKLED UP THE RIDE AIN'T OVER...Much more turbulence ahead!

Here I am trying to be a mother along with trying to balance my womanhood, after the demise of my relationship with Tyrese's dad. I thought that bouncing back into the dating scene would be easy breezy for me, being that I still had my MOJO, my attractiveness and my zeal for a better life.

But! I was wrong.

A decade or so had past since my last relationship. The dating journey was absolutely horrible. I had countless interaction with people that meant me absolutely no good. I was still running around trying to find someone to love on and validate me. I was still searching for those fantasies that I was so engulfed in on television. When I say when you're haunted by so much trauma, this is the path that's prone to happen. I was chasing a love that didn't love me back. If you haven't address your traumatic issues that haunted you everyday of your life, you'll try to seek validation from anything or anyone to fill in the empty wholes in your heart. That is exactly what I did for very long time of my life. I WANT SOMEONE TO SEE! The equation of LUST had become the common denominator to the source of my painful dating journey. I was connecting with souls that were just as damaged as I was. The more I encountered those ILLEGAL SOUL TIES, the more my soul started to encounter some demonic exchanges.

GOD TAKE ME AWAY FROM THESE HAUNTED CONNECTIONS THATS KILLING MY SOUL!

My mind, body and soul was EXHAUSTED. I want to start chasing something else other than these men. I want to KILL the FLESH within me, that was leading my life into pure SELF DESTRUCTION. I wanted to chase this entity that I could feel around me at times. I could feel that there was something BIGGER than me, that could help me see the GLORY outside my pain and dysfunction.

That Desire, That Feeling and That Entity was...GOD!

GOD WAS GETTING READY TO SHOW ME BETTER THAN HE COULD TELL ME!

Let the healing Begin...

God was dismantling me brick by brick so that he could REBUILD me slowly into a better version of me..

But! My FLESH had to be cleaned out some more and that cleansing process was more than a notion.

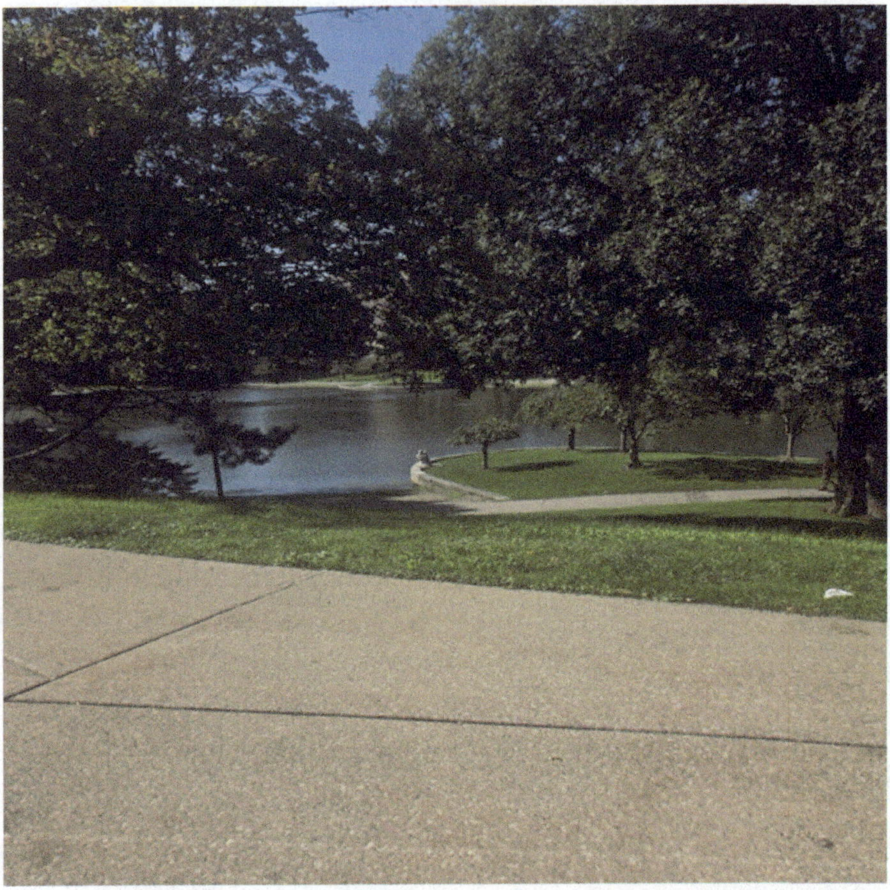

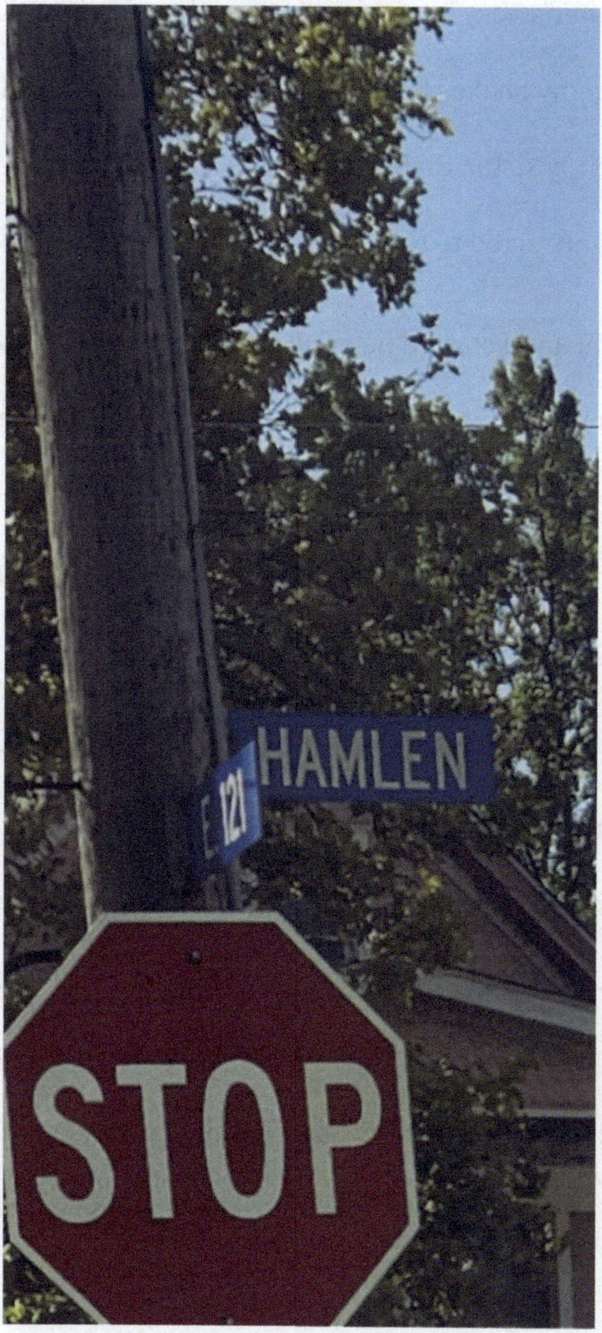
HAMLEN
E. 121
STOP

So after a very long time of being alone I met a person that I knew from my Shaker Heights neighborhood. He actually went to school with my sister, therefore, he was a little younger than me (I was always attracted to the young ones). His name was Kevin.

Kevin and I started hanging out on a regular basis. I enjoyed him a lot, for the simple fact that he seemed SAFE. He wasn't like those street guys that I had previously engaged with. I felt relaxed with him. He was different. He wasn't LOUD! I need the quietness that he carried with him.

After dating on and off for a few years I started to put on the pressures of marriage because now I'm in church on a regular, which led me to become an ordained deaconess. The pressures of living a certain way were starting to infiltrate my ears. Even though I started seeing turmoil and dysfunction showing up in our relationship, I swept those signs under the rug, and stay on my mission to create my own family with Kevin. In the interim we had

3 children (we lost our first son at birth) that was DEVASTATING and horrific. That Loss was something that I never thought I would experience. Now I have two boys along with their older brother, Tyrese.

Slowly but surely the walls of the home were starting to be haunted with some familiar sounds of the dysfunctions of his life along with haunted sounds of the dysfunctions of my life.

See his dysfunction was not loud, so that's why I thought that I was safe with him. My dysfunction is obviously very loud! No matter how quiet or how loud dysfunction sounds it still HOLLERS DYSFUNCTION.

Our home front together was becoming increasingly LOUD was the haunting noises of chaos and hurt, slowly affected our children. THERE WERE NOT TOO MANY HARMONIOUS moments being developed in our house, to add insult to injury, we got MARRIED. I was too prideful to back out of the nuptials. The lies of dysfunction convinced me that things were going to get better... NOT TRUE AT ALL! Things actually got worse. By the time we said I DO, I had checked out way before. Mentally, sexually and emotionally, I was disconnected, depressed and numb from all the pain that we all were going through within the walls of our home. I NEED TO HEAL GOD...THIS IS NOT FOR ME...GOD HELP ME!

It's time to Let Go and Go Heal!

I didn't know how or when, but in my heart I was counting down to my exit of a marriage that wasn't conducive to Kevin, my children or myself. Each day that I was in that home and with him, I WAS SLOWLY LOSING ME!...stuck between staying to keep my family together and leaving (REMEMBER I TOLD YOU ALL THE LIES DYSFUNCTION WHISPERS IN YOUR EAR). My kids were suffering, I needed a way out!

GODS EXITS...

After being together a total of almost eighteen years (with

one year of marriage) finally, God gave me and my boys an exit to step through. God had pointed to many exits, I was too fearful to step through it. There was something about this exit. It felt right, so on October 5, 2011 I packed two trash bags of my children's clothing, I didn't even take my any of my clothes, only my work scrubs and we made our exit.

I stepped right out that exit right into the ENTRANCE OF MY HEALING. That day a load of bricks that held my shoulders down for many, many years starting falling to the floor one by one. I didn't know how I was going to make it happen, but what I knew was that as long as God was walking right beside me that everything was going to work out for my good and it did glory hallelujah!

Here I am finally at the door of my healing process. I couldn't wait to face and start healing from the demons that HAUNTED my life for so long. GOD HAD TO START THE EXORCISM process over my HAUNTED and TRAUMA filled life.

The exorcism was not or is not an easy process, God stripped me down to the bare minimum, God had to show and reveal somethings to me. He started revealing the secrets and lies of my journey. Like being kidnapped as a child. Showing the true face of those around me by stripping the mask off of people who claimed to love me. God started revealing my family's ugly and distorted secrets and lies, MY LORD!

I started healing me. I was able to start seeing things through a pair of healing eyes, GLORY!

As God heals me, I start addressing my family hurt and generational curses.

As God heals me, I started addressing my friendship and family hurt and disappointment.

As God heals me, my children were able to get the help that they needed. GLORY TO GOD!

Oooh! The ride to healing hasn't been easy. Healing is an ongoing process. I Thank God that I stayed buckled up to continue my journey to peace and healing HALLELUJAH!

Even though it is still revealing something to me, I can PROUDLY say those HAUNTED noises that once crept through every wall of my homes are slowly DYING DOWN! GLORY TO GOD! Trust me when I tell you there is still work to be done on me but thanks to God for bringing me this far. The old and painful skin that I once wore is slowly but surely being replaced with JOY, HAPPINESS and PEACE and I want to marinate in it as much as I can, REST IN PEACE WHEN I'M DEAD!? Nawl! I'm RESTING IN PEACE NOW.

God ain't done with me YET! For I have work to do for his Kingdom.

God is not done with YOU YET! Stay the course to your peace.

Fight for your Healing!

GOD TOOK A WRETCH LIKE ME AND HE'S USING ME! Hallelujah!

People counted me out and GOD CONNECTED ME IN! GLORY!

Here I stand...

Minister Tracy S. Knox

Mother

Grandmother

Author

Speaker

And a woman of God

This was all God's plans for me, and it came with a painful price just like God's only begotten Son .... HALLELUJAH

Remember Healing is Essential and IT'S FREE!

I'm Praying for you all! Amen

This is my Story; this is my Testimony and God is the Author of it All.


Stay Tuned.

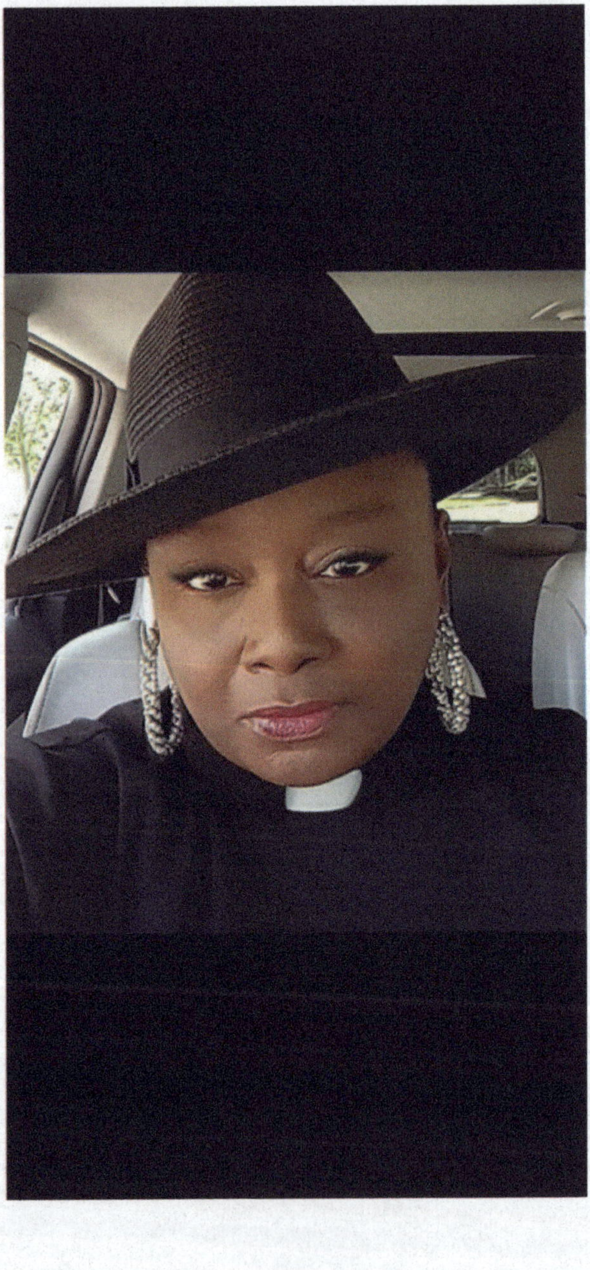

Made in the USA
Columbia, SC
08 February 2025